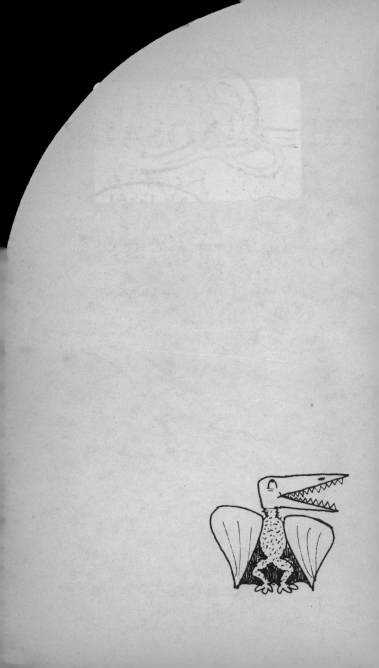

THE DINOSAUR JOKE BOOK

by Terry Dactyl

illustrated by Andy Cunningham

A Piccolo Original
Piccolo Books

First published 1989 by Pan Books Ltd,
Cavaye Place, London SW10 9PG

9 8 7 6 5 4 3 2 1

© Terry Dactyl 1989

Illustrations © Andy Cunningham 1989

ISBN 0 330 30846 7

Phototypeset by Input Typesetting Ltd, London

Printed and bound in Great Britain
by Richard Clay Ltd, Bungay, Suffolk

Dinosaurs

Dinosaurs were a group of reptiles that lived on Earth from about 200 million years ago to about 65 million years ago – long before the first people appeared on the planet. Until about 150 years ago, no one even knew that dinosaurs had existed!

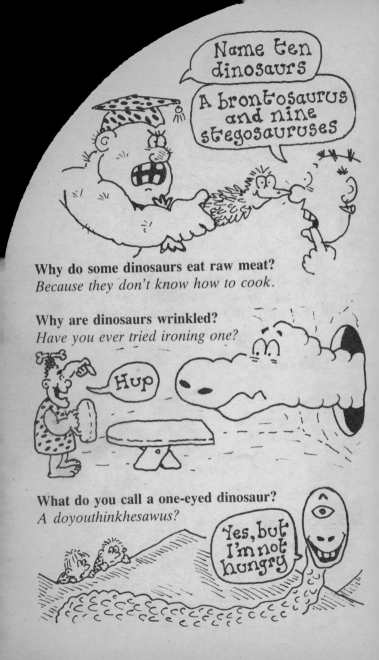

Why do some dinosaurs eat raw meat?
Because they don't know how to cook.

Why are dinosaurs wrinkled?
Have you ever tried ironing one?

What do you call a one-eyed dinosaur?
A doyouthinkhesawus?

Where do you find dinosaurs?
It depends where you leave them.

What were the very first drains called?

Dinosewers

What brings baby dinosaurs?
Enormous storks.

In prehistoric times, what did they call disasters at sea?
Tyrannosaurus wrecks.

Nobody knows what colour dinosaurs were, or whether they had stripes, spots or any sort of markings at all.

What do you get if you cross a dinosaur with a kangaroo?
Big holes across Australia.

Did you know, some dinosaurs were so tall they had to stand on a chair to brush their teeth?

What do you get if you cross a dinosaur with a dog?
Terrified postmen.

What do you get if you cross a dinosaur with a worm?
Big holes in the garden.

What do you get if you cross a dinosaur with a hedgehog?

What do you get if you cross a dinosaur with a cow?
I don't know, but you have to stand up to milk it.

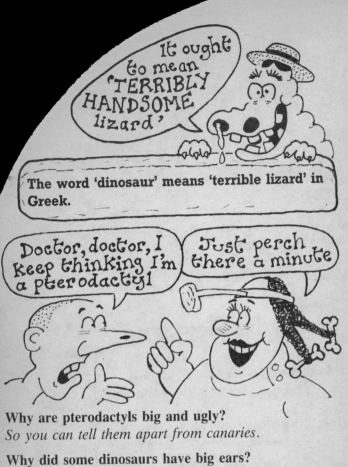

The word 'dinosaur' means 'terrible lizard' in Greek.

Why are pterodactyls big and ugly?
So you can tell them apart from canaries.

Why did some dinosaurs have big ears?
Because Noddy wouldn't pay the ransom.

What do you get if you cross a lemon with a dinosaur?
A dino-sour.

What do you do with a green dinosaur?
Wait until it ripens.

What do you do with a blue dinosaur?
Try to cheer it up.

What's yellow and highly dangerous?
Brontosaurus-infested custard.

Why don't dinosaurs have balls?
Because they're not very good dancers.

How do dinosaurs find each other in the long grass?

Knock, knock.
Who's there?
Olive.
Olive who?
Olive in that cave over there.

Who lost a herd of dinosaurs?
Big Bo Peep.

Why do pterodactyls fly south for the winter?

Because they don't know how to swim

What is the best way to catch a dinosaur?
Ask someone to throw it to you.

No!

What has two wheels and weighs six tons?
A dinosaur on a motorbike.

Why do some dinosaurs have such long necks?
Because their feet smell.

How do you make a dinosaur fly?
Buy it an airline ticket.

Why do dinosaurs have wrinkled ankles?
Because they lace their boots too tightly.

What's huge and wrinkled and red all over?

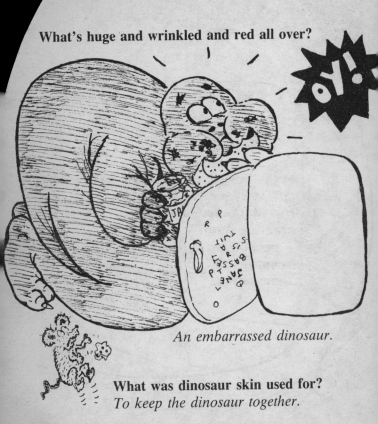

An embarrassed dinosaur.

What was dinosaur skin used for?
To keep the dinosaur together.

What did the psychiatrist charge the dinosaur?
£10 for the visit, and £150 for a new couch.

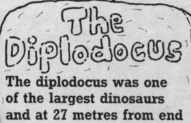

The Diplodocus

The diplodocus was one of the largest dinosaurs and at 27 metres from end to end, the longest land creature ever! It was a vegetarian and must have spent nearly all its time eating.

VEGGY-BURGERS

Not true! I spend **ALL** my (chomp) time eating

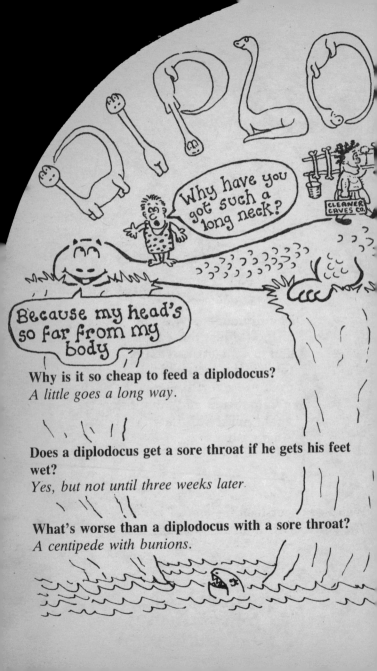

Why have you got such a long neck?

Because my head's so far from my body

Why is it so cheap to feed a diplodocus?
A little goes a long way.

Does a diplodocus get a sore throat if he gets his feet wet?
Yes, but not until three weeks later.

What's worse than a diplodocus with a sore throat?
A centipede with bunions.

What do you get if you cross a glow-worm with a diplodocus?
A 72-foot strip light.

What do you get if you cross a racehorse with a diplodocus?
An animal that's difficult to ride but great in a photo-finish.

Which dinosaur took the longest to apologize?
The diplodocus. It took him a long time to swallow his pride.

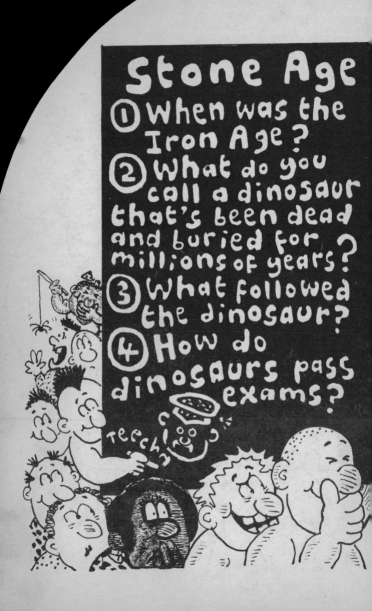

History Test
Arnsurs
① Before The invenshun of drip Dry shurts
② Pete (eesy)
③ Its Eail
④ Wiv extinction

The largest dinosaur egg ever found was the size of a rugby ball and was discovered in France.

What happens when dinosaurs hold beauty contests?

A dinosaur walks in some mud and makes huge footprints, then it rains. Which member of the Royal Family does that remind you of?

How do you know when there's a dinosaur in your bed?
Your nose is touching the ceiling.

How do you know when there's a brontosaurus in your bed?
It's got a 'B' on its pyjamas.

What's huge and wrinkled and jumps every two seconds?
A dinosaur with hiccoughs.

Why do dinosaurs scratch themselves?
Because they're the only ones who know where they itch.

The largest prehistoric fish, the carcharodon megalodon, was the size of a lorry and could open its jaws so wide that four adult humans could have stood in its mouth.

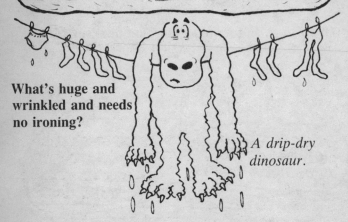

What's huge and wrinkled and needs no ironing?

A drip-dry dinosaur.

What is the difference between a wet day and a dinosaur with toothache?
One is pouring with rain, the other is roaring with pain.

A dinosaur lady of Thrace,
Had a nose covering half of her face;
She'd very few kisses,
The reason for this is
There wasn't a suitable place.

How do you get fur from a dinosaur?
Run fast in the opposite direction!

Knock, knock.
Who's there?
Iguana.
Iguana who?
Iguana hold your hand.

Knock, knock.
Who's there?
Dragon.
Dragon who?
Dragon your feet again.

What's huge and wrinkled and goes thump-squish, thump-squish?
A dinosaur with one wet plimsoll.

How do you make a dinosaur sandwich?
First, you take a VERY big loaf . . .

What's the difference between a dinosaur and an egg?
Have you ever tried scrambling a dinosaur?

What's huge and black and delicious?
A chocolate-covered dinosaur.

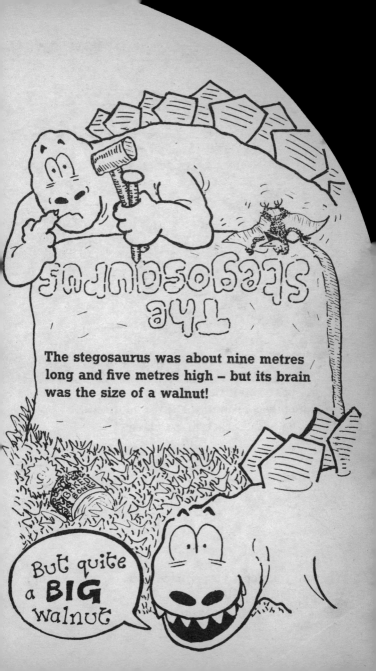

The Stegosaurus

The stegosaurus was about nine metres long and five metres high – but its brain was the size of a walnut!

But quite a **BIG** walnut

Did you hear about the stegosaurus who chased a daddy long legs around for three hours, then realized he had a crack in his glasses?

What do you get if you replace a stegosaurus's mind with an elastic band?
A real stretch of the imagination.

with the circus? The police made him bring it back!

Did you hear about the stegosaurus who bought a sleeping bag?

He spent two months trying to wake it up.

What a lazy-bones!

How can you tell a stegosaurus's age?

Cut off the top of its head and count the rings.

Did you hear about the stegosaurus who bought a new tie?
He took it back the next day and complained that it was too tight.

Did you hear about the stegosaurus who tried to walk around the world?
He drowned.

Why was the stegosaurus using a calculator?
To count how many legs he had.

Why was the stegosaurus jumping up and down?
He'd taken some medicine and forgotten to shake the bottle.

Why did the stegosaurus have a flat head?
From chasing parked cars.

Did you hear about the stegosaurus who was teaching his dog to wee in the gutter?
He fell off the roof.

YAH!

Did you hear about the stegosaurus who went to the mind-reader?
What do you get if you cross a stegosaurus with a pair of glasses?
An idiot who keeps making a spectacle of himself
HA HA HA HA
HE HE HE HO
HA HA
I wonder what all my friends down there are laughing about

Tyrannosaurus rex was the deadliest dinosaur. It had sharp, curved teeth the size of kitchen knives!

What's huge and wrinkled and smells?
A dinosaur's nose.

There was a young caveman called Fisher,
Who was fishing for fish in a fissure;
When a cod, with a grin,
Pulled the fisherman in,
Now they're fishing the fissure for Fisher.

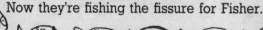

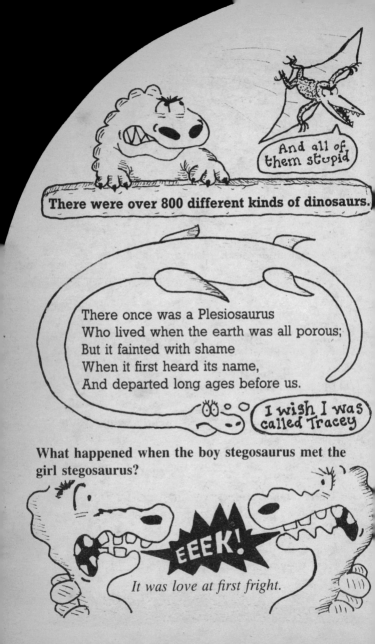

And all of them stupid

There were over 800 different kinds of dinosaurs.

There once was a Plesiosaurus
Who lived when the earth was all porous;
But it fainted with shame
When it first heard its name,
And departed long ages before us.

I wish I was called Tracey

What happened when the boy stegosaurus met the girl stegosaurus?

EEEK!

It was love at first fright.

What do you get if you cross a dinosaur with a witch?
A tyrannosaurus hex.

What do you get if you cross a dinosaur with a cactus?
The biggest porcupine in the world.

What do you get if you cross a teddy bear with a dinosaur?
I don't know, but I wouldn't try cuddling it.

What do you get if you cross a dinosaur with locusts?
I don't know, but if they swarm, watch out!

What's the difference between a dead bee and a sick dinosaur?
One is a bee deceased, the other is a seedy beast.

A large sailing ship was at anchor off Mauritius. Two dodos watched from the bushes as a boatload of sailors rowed ashore. 'Quick, let's go and hide,' said the first dodo. 'Why?' asked the other. 'Because we're supposed to be extinct, silly!'

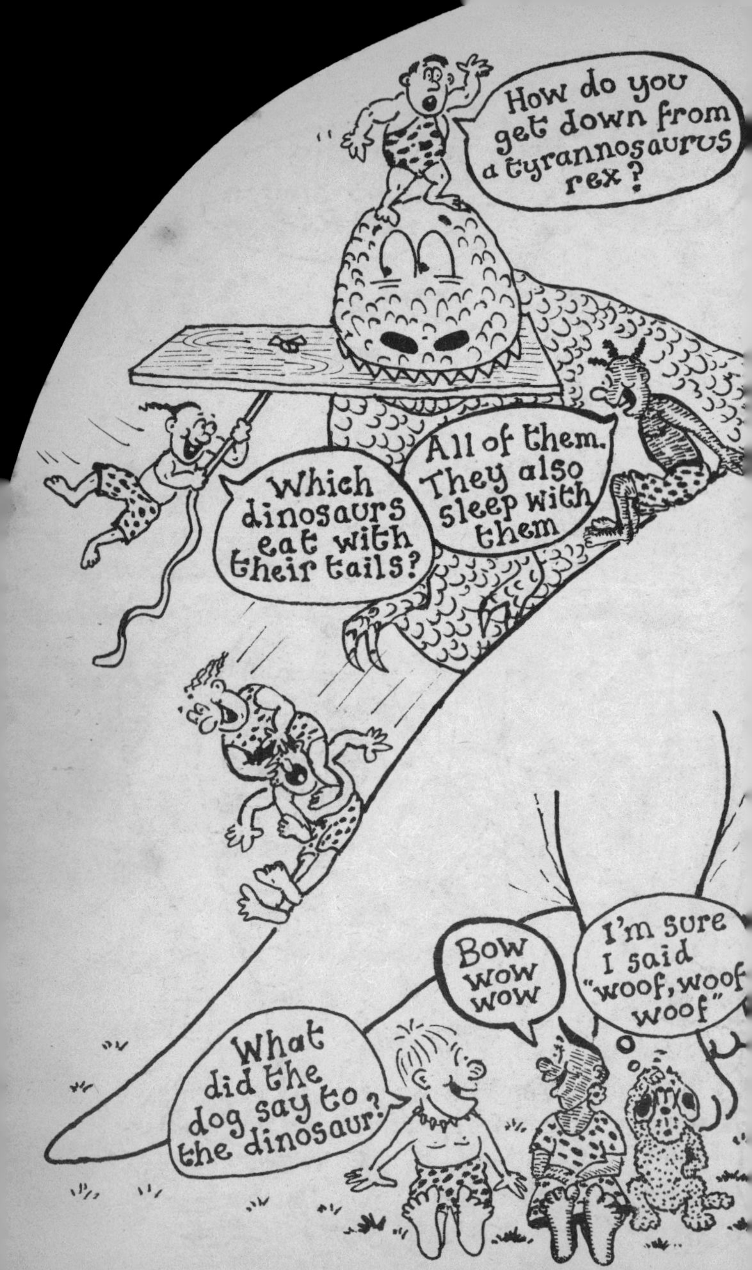
How do you get down from a tyrannosaurus rex?
Which dinosaurs eat with their tails?
All of them. They also sleep with them
What did the dog say to the dinosaur?
Bow wow wow
I'm sure I said "woof, woof woof"

Reptiles were the first animals with backbones who were able to live entirely on land.

What is an archaeologist?
A person whose career is in ruins.

What kind of dates do archaeologists go out with?
Anyone they can dig up.

What do you call a dinosaur at the North Pole?

What do you give a seasick dinosaur?

plenty of room!

What do you call a carriage-load of struthiomimuses on the underground?

A tube of smarties.

Did you hear about the struthiomimus who ran a two-minute mile?
He found a short cut.

How do you run over a brontosaurus?
Dash up its tail, sprint along

How do you stop a dinosaur from charging?
Take away his credit card.

What's huge and wrinkled and good at sums?
A dinosaur with a calculator.

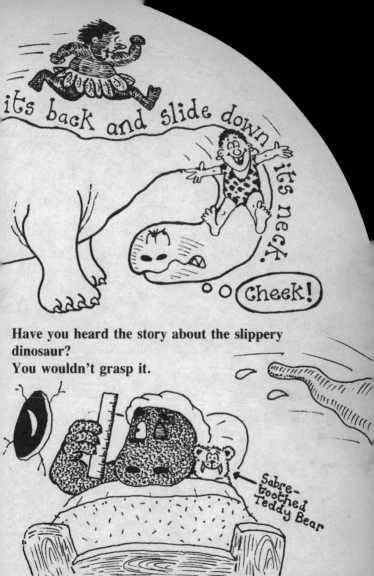

its back and slide down its neck.

Cheek!

Have you heard the story about the slippery
dinosaur?
You wouldn't grasp it.

Sabre-
toothed
Teddy Bear

Why did the dinosaur take a ruler to bed with him?
To find out how long he slept.

The largest dinosaur footprints ever found, in Texas, are so huge that each can hold as much water as a bath.

What do you get if you cross a dinosaur with a kangaroo?
Flat Australians.

What do you get if you cross a dinosaur with a skunk?

What do you get if you cross a dinosaur with a canary?
A very messy cage.

What kind of umbrellas do dinosaurs use in heavy rain?
Wet ones.

What's worse than a dinosaur on waterskis?
A porcupine on a rubber life raft.

What ballet is most popular with dinosaurs?

What do you get if you cross a dinosaur with a pigeon?

Lots of very worried pedestrians!

What is huge and wrinkled and wears a mask?
The Lone Dinosaur.

What do you get if you cross a dinosaur with a pig?
Very large pork chops.

Why did dinosaurs have thick, wrinkly skins?
They'd have looked silly in plastic macs, wouldn't they?

What do dinosaurs have that no other animal has?
Baby dinosaurs.

Why don't brontosauruses grow any longer?
Because they're long enough already.

Did you hear about the dinosaur who stayed up all night trying to work out what happened to the sun when it went down?

It finally dawned on him.

What's the best way to raise a baby dinosaur?
In a fork-lift truck.

Which dinosaurs have their eyes closest together?

The smallest ones.

What's the difference between a dinosaur and a biscuit?
Ever tried dunking a dinosaur?

What do you get if you cross a dinosaur with peanut butter?
A dinosaur that sticks to the roof of your mouth.

What's the difference between a dinosaur and a sandwich?
A sandwich doesn't usually weigh 7 tons.

Why don't dinosaurs eat penguins?
Because they can't get the wrappers off.

How does a dinosaur get up an oak tree?
It sits on an acorn and waits for it to grow.

How does a dinosaur escape when it's stuck up a tree?
It waits for autumn and floats down on a leaf.

What did dinosaurs say when they bumped into each other?

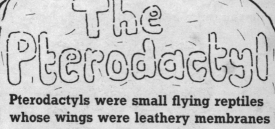

The Pterodactyl

Pterodactyls were small flying reptiles whose wings were leathery membranes stretched over very long arms and fingers. They probably rested hanging upside down. They had lots of very sharp teeth.

AH!

Terror with a capital "P"

Where do the toughest pterodactyls come from?
Hard-boiled eggs.

What do you call a pterodactyl with no beak?
A headbanger.

What is a pterodactyl's favourite TV programme?
The feather forecast.

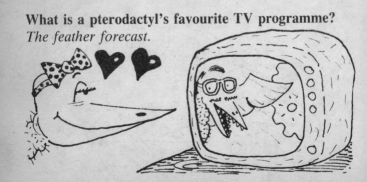

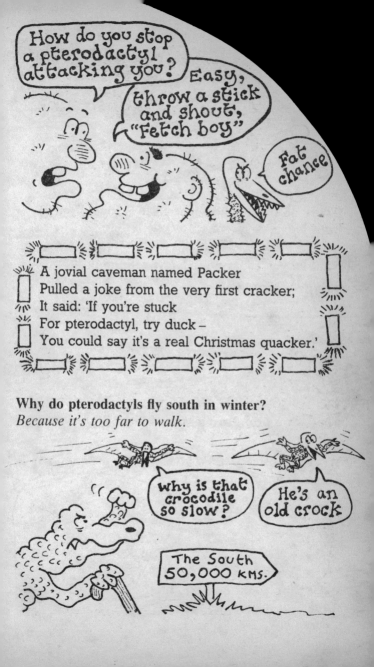

A jovial caveman named Packer
Pulled a joke from the very first cracker;
It said: 'If you're stuck
For pterodactyl, try duck –
You could say it's a real Christmas quacker.'

Why do pterodactyls fly south in winter?
Because it's too far to walk.

What has a beak, two legs, and flies?

What is ugly and blue and flies?
A pterodactyl holding its breath.

Why is the sky so high?
So the pterodactyls won't bang their heads.

Why couldn't the pterodactyl talk to the dove?
Because he didn't speak pigeon English.

How do we know pterodactyls are religious?
Because they are birds of prey.

What is ugly and flies and wears sunglasses?
A pterodactyl on holiday.

100 years ago in Wyoming, USA, a man found so many huge bones that he built himself a cabin using 500 of them. It wasn't until much later that he found out they were dinosaur bones . . .

Two dinosaurs fell over a cliff – boom, boom!'

Is it difficult to bury a dinosaur?
Yes, it's a huge undertaking.

Why is a dinosaur's tooth eleven inches long?
If it was any longer, it would be a foot.

Knock, knock.
Who's there?
Ben.
Ben who?
Ben a long time since dinosaurs were on the earth.

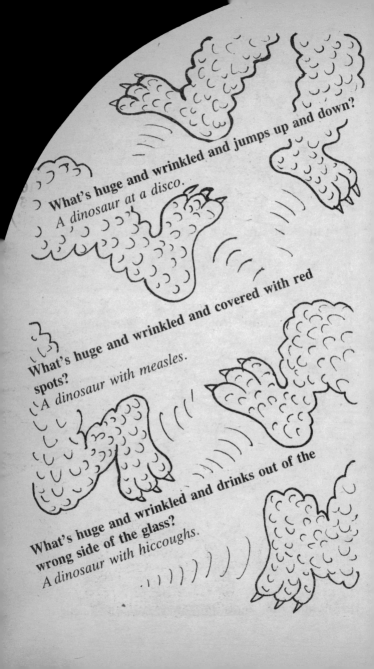

What's huge and wrinkled and jumps up and down?
A dinosaur at a disco.

What's huge and wrinkled and covered with red spots?
A dinosaur with measles.

What's huge and wrinkled and drinks out of the wrong side of the glass?
A dinosaur with hiccoughs.

Why did dinosaurs wear sandals?
To stop their feet sinking into the sand.

Why did prehistoric ostriches bury their heads in the sand?
To see if the dinosaurs were wearing sandals.

Why did the dinosaur chase its tail?
It was trying to make ends meet.

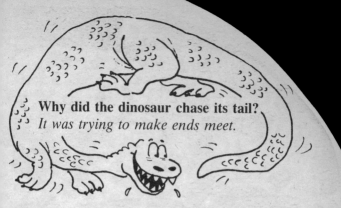

Why don't you ever see dinosaurs in the zoo?
They can't afford to buy a ticket.

What do you get if you cross a dinosaur with a boy scout?

Where did the go when he lost his tail?
To the retail shop
Why does the have a trunk?
Because he doesn't have a glove compartment
What did you do if your was stolen?
Call the flying squad
'Course they can
These jokes were old when I was a boy
How do you scold a ?
Tusk tusk

What do you do if a tyrannosaurus sits in front of you at the cinema?
Miss most of the film!

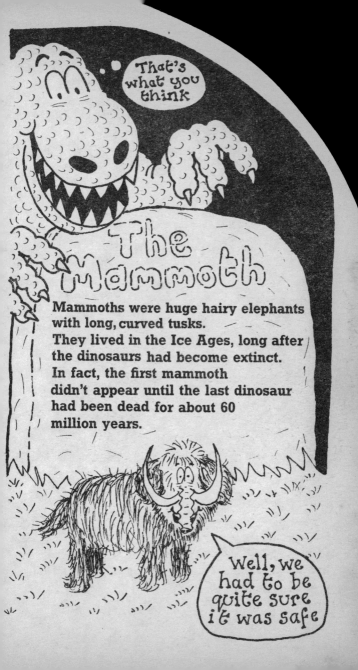

The Mammoth

Mammoths were huge hairy elephants with long, curved tusks.
They lived in the Ice Ages, long after the dinosaurs had become extinct.
In fact, the first mammoth didn't appear until the last dinosaur had been dead for about 60 million years.

Ten mammoths
nother mammoth's tail?
What are you trying to do?
None – mammoths can't talk!

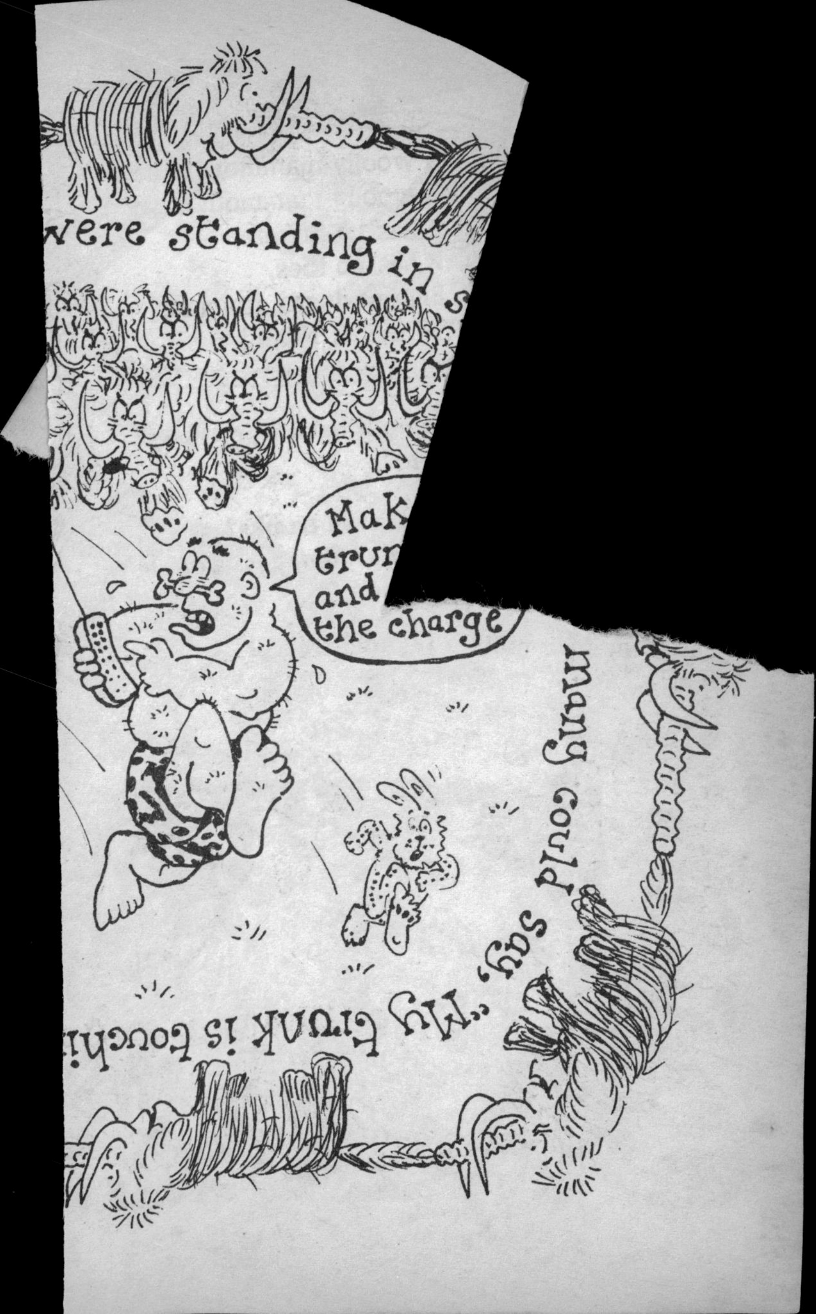

...moth is huge,
...is fat;

...ingle File. How

...e a
...K call
...verse
...bags, wouldn't

...hat is the mammoth's favourite carol?
'The Holly and the Ivory.'

♪ The Holly and the Ivory ♪

What is the mammoth's favourite football team?
Trunkmere Rovers.

Where do woolly mammoths go for their holidays?
Tuskany.

How do woolly mammoths have a bath?
They take their trunks off.

How do you make a mammoth fly?
Start with a six-foot zip . . .

What do woolly mammoths learn at school?
Mammothematics.

Why is a prehistoric elephant like a female butterfly?
Because it is a ma-moth.

How do you keep a woolly mammoth from smelling?
Tie a knot in its trunk.

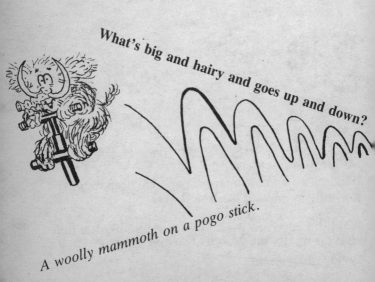

Knock, knock.
Who's there?
Tusk.
Tusk who?
Tusk you to be nosey.

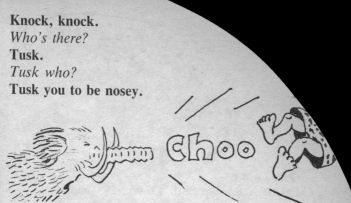

What's the best thing to do when a woolly mammoth has a blocked nose?
Run like crazy if he sneezes.

What's got four ears, eight legs, two tails, four eyes and two trunks?
A woolly mammoth with spare parts.

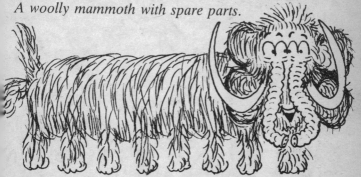

What do you call a metre-high woolly mammoth?
Trunkated.

What did cavemen need to spot a mammoth a mile away?
Very good icesight.

What was the ice mammoth's favourite food?
Iceburgers.

Why was it difficult to keep a secret in the Ice Age?
Because your teeth chattered so much.

How did cavemen go to work in the Ice Age?
By icicle.

What do you get if you cross an ice mammoth with a dinosaur?
A jumbo yeti.

How did cavemen dress in the Ice Age?

Quickly!

What did the ice mammoth hum to himself while he was dancing?
'Snow, snow, thick, thick snow.'

What do you call a dinosaur in the Ice Age?
A cold snap.

What has two wings and gives money to baby mammoths?
The tusk fairy.

What's worse than a dinosaur with a stiff neck?
A woolly mammoth with a stuffed nose.

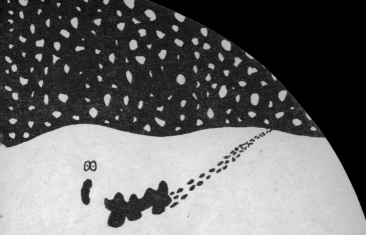

What goes out black and comes back white?
A black woolly mammoth in a snowstorm.

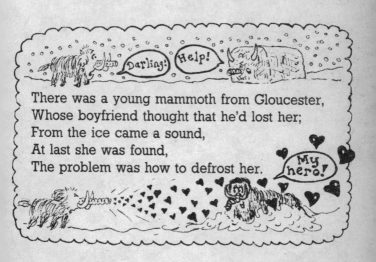

There was a young mammoth from Gloucester,
Whose boyfriend thought that he'd lost her;
From the ice came a sound,
At last she was found,
The problem was how to defrost her.

What is big and hairy and sees just as well from either end?
A woolly mammoth with its eyes shut.

What's huge and wrinkled and loves pepperoni pizza?

An Italian dinosaur.

What's as big as a dinosaur but weighs nothing?
A dinosaur's shadow.

Knock, knock.
Who's there?
Dinosaur.
Dinosaur who?
Dinosaur with you because you called her stupid.

What's huge and wrinkled and goes bleep-bleep?
A dinosaur in a traffic jam.

What's huge and wrinkled, has eight legs, and whinnies?
A dinosaur on a horse.

What's huge and wrinkled and has eight wheels?
A dinosaur on roller skates.

Hello little cousin

About 65 million years ago, all the dinosaurs disappeared from the face of the Earth. But not all their relatives died out – the crocodile is a living cousin of the dinosaurs.

What's the first thing a dinosaur does if it breaks a toe?
Give up ballet.

Knock, knock.
Who's there?
Thea.
Thea who?
Thea later, alligator.

Knock. knock.
Who's there?
Lucretia.
Lucretia who?
Lucretia from the primeval swamp.

How long should a dinosaur's legs be?
Long enough to reach the ground.

Why is the dinosaur's nose in the middle of its face?
Because it's the scenter.

What did the stegosaurus say when it was bitten by a snake?
Nothing: stegosauruses can't talk.

What goes 'Ha, ha, bonk'?
A dinosaur laughing his head off.

What's extinct and works in rodeos?
A bucking bronco-saurus.